525542

3 2222 0060 4852 6

J

8/12

CITY CRITTERS

YOUR NEIGHBOR THE PIGEON

GREG ROZA

WINDMILL
BOOKS ™

New York

Published in 2012 by Windmill Books, An Imprint of Rosen Publishing
29 East 21st Street, New York, NY 10010

First Edition

Editor: Jennifer Way
Layout Design: Greg Tucker

Photo Credits: Cover, pp. 4, 5, 6, 7, 8, 9, 11 (top, bottom), 12, 13, 16 (top, bottom), 17,18, 19 (top), 20, 22 Shutterstock.com; pp. 10, 14, 15, 21 iStockphoto/Thinkstock; p. 19 (bottom) Comstock/Thinkstock.

Library of Congress Cataloging-in-Publication Data

Roza, Greg.
 Your neighbor the pigeon / by Greg Roza. — 1st ed.
   p. cm. — (City critters)
 Includes bibliographical references and index.
 ISBN 978-1-61533-384-4 (library binding : alk. paper) — ISBN 978-1-4488-5133-1 (pbk. : alk. paper) — ISBN 978-1-4488-5134-8 (6-pack)
 1. Pigeons—Juvenile literature. I. Title. II. Series.
 QL696.C63R69 2012
 598.6'5—dc22

                                         2011001851

Manufactured in the United States of America

For more great fiction and nonfiction, go to www.windmillbooks.com

CPSIA Compliance Information: Batch #BS2011WM: For Further Information contact Windmill Books, New York, New York at 1-866-478-0556

CONTENTS

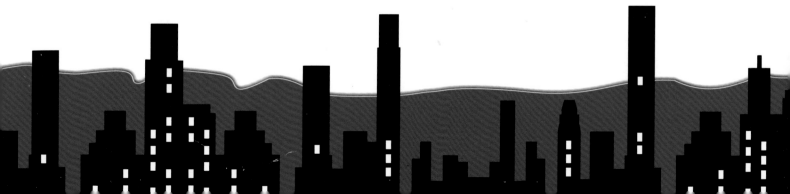

BIRDS IN THE CITY

Pigeons live all over the world. Many live in the wild, but many others live in towns and cities. In the wild, pigeons like to make their homes on tall cliffs. Those that live in towns and cities often make their nests on building ledges.

In many cities, pigeons are a common sight.

Sometimes people leave out breadcrumbs to draw pigeons. This draws big groups of the birds!

Some people like pigeons. They may keep them as pets. However, many people who live in cities think pigeons are pests. They make messes and carry illnesses. This book will teach you more about these common city critters.

More than 300 kinds of doves and pigeons belong to the scientific family of birds called Columbidae. The pigeons people see in cities are mostly rock pigeons. The rock pigeon is the main kind of pigeon discussed in this book.

The Mesopotamians first **domesticated** pigeons about 6,500 years ago.

Pigeons are known for being able to find their way home over long distances. This is called homing. People have used domesticated pigeons for races as well as to send messages.

Over the years, pigeons have been prized for their excellent **homing** abilities. They were first brought to North America in the early 1600s. They quickly spread across the country. Today, they can be found from southern Canada all the way down to the southern tip of South America.

Rock pigeons are found in North America, South America, Europe, and in parts of Asia, Australia, and Africa.

PIGEON FOOD

In the wild, rock pigeons eat mostly seeds and grains that they find on the ground. These include corn, oats, and wheat. They will also eat leaves, fruit, bugs, and worms.

In towns and cities, pigeons are known to eat just about anything people throw

City pigeons will eat all kinds of human foods. These pigeons are eating corn.

away. They will dig through garbage cans or eat food off the ground. They like popcorn, french fries, bread, peanuts, and many other foods people have thrown away. Pigeons often gather in parks where people feed them breadcrumbs. City pigeons will even follow people who are eating, hoping they will drop something.

Pigeons are not the only city birds that eat food left behind by people. This pigeon (right) might have to share a bit of bread with a group of sparrows!

ADULT PIGEONS

Adult rock pigeons generally have bluish gray feathers on their heads, necks, and chests. Most have light gray wings with two dark bands on them and one dark band on the tail. Many have **iridescent** patches on their heads and necks. However, pigeons' body colors can vary from white to brown to black.

Like other birds, pigeons sit on their eggs to keep them warm.

Left: These are pigeon eggs. The eggs hatch after 17 to 19 days. Bottom: Here is a female (left) and a male (right) pigeon.

Unlike many animals, pigeons **mate** for life. Females lay one or two eggs four to five times a year. The male makes the nest on a high ledge and guards the female. Both parents sit on the eggs. They also both help feed their young.

11

SQUABS

Young pigeons are called squabs. They do not eat seeds, as adults do. Pigeon parents feed their squabs a thick, milky liquid that they make in their **crops**. Squabs reach adulthood in four to six weeks. By this time, the female may have

The liquid that pigeon parents feed their squabs is called crop milk. Crop milk helps squabs, like the ones shown here, grow quickly.

laid more eggs in the nest, so it might be a little crowded!

Pigeons raised in **captivity** may live 15 years or longer. This is because they have steady supplies of food, safe shelter, and no enemies. City pigeons, however, do not often live more than 3 or 4 years.

Pigeons can mate throughout the year. Most babies are born during the spring and summer, though.

AT HOME WITH PIGEONS

The wild rock pigeon is native to Europe, southwestern Asia, and northern Africa. These birds generally live high up, especially on cliffs. They make loose, messy nests. Pigeons are social birds that are often found in large groups, called flights or flocks.

City pigeon look for clifflike places to build their nests. They often build nests in and around air conditioners.

The rock pigeons of North America are **feral** birds. This means that they were once domesticated animals but have since returned to the wild. Just like their wild cousins, feral pigeons like to nest in high clifflike places. Building ledges, rafters, bridges, and chimneys make the best **urban** homes.

Here is a wild pigeon nesting in a hole in a cliff.

PIGEONS IN YOUR NEIGHBORHOOD

City pigeons are not shy about gathering near cafés and parks where people are eating!

Look up when you are walking down the street. Do you see nests on building ledges? They are likely pigeon nests.

Be careful! Pigeons are known to drop their waste as they fly!

Anyone who lives in a city will tell you that pigeon droppings are a real pain! Not only do they make messes, but they also harm buildings, statues, and car paint.

Although pigeons can be messy, they clean city sidewalks by eating crumbs and other leftovers people drop.

Pigeon feathers can build up where they live. You may also see their eggshells.

People who keep pigeons as pets often keep them in rooftop cages.

Pigeons have not just **adapted** to city life, they thrive in it. This is partly due to the fact that they **reproduce** quickly. Pigeons in cities have fewer enemies than pigeons in the wild. Food is generally plentiful.

Aside from illnesses, people are city pigeons' biggest enemy. Some people put out sharp things to keep them

Many people do not want pigeons roosting on their buildings. They do things to keep pigeons away or to harm them.

Left: The red-tailed hawk is a predator of pigeons in the wild. *Bottom*: Some cat owners let their cats outside. Cats will chase and sometimes kill birds like pigeons.

from **roosting** on their windowsills. Some people use traps to catch pigeons. Others use cats to chase pigeons away. Some people dislike pigeons so much they put out poisoned food or even shoot them. Doing these things is illegal in most places.

PETS OR PESTS?

Many people who study history believe that pigeons were the first birds to be domesticated. They have been used to carry messages over long distances for centuries. Today, some people like to keep them as pets. Pigeons have even been used for food and scientific studies.

Pigeons often stop to rest on statues. Their droppings are messy and smelly, and they carry germs. They may harm buildings or statues, too.

Many people who live in towns and cities hate the messes pigeons make. Pigeon droppings have germs in them that can make people sick. There is not a great chance you will get sick, but it is still a bad idea, and gross, to touch pigeon droppings.

People who keep pigeons as pets may have several of them. They may keep their cages on the roof of a building.

URBAN SAFARI

Pigeons are found in nearly every city in the United States. They are generally very easy to spot.

If you have pigeons in your neighborhood, you are sure to find signs of them even when you do not see them gathering in a large group. They often roost on high ledges. You will also see them on roofs, chimneys, and barns. You are

These pigeons have made their home in a drain pipe.

sure to find their droppings, especially under their favorite roosting spots. You will likely also find their gray feathers. Going on an urban safari can be a good way to learn more about city pigeons.

GLOSSARY

ADAPTED (uh-DAPT-ed) Changed to fit new conditions.

CAPTIVITY (kap-TIH-vih-tee) A place where animals live, such as in a home, a zoo, or an aquarium, instead of living in the wild.

CROPS (KROPS) Sacs inside the necks of birds where food is stored.

DOMESTICATED (duh-MES-tih-kayt-ed) Raised to live with people.

FERAL (FER-al) An animal that used to live with people but that has gone back to the wild.

HOMING (HOHM-ing) Finding one's way home after traveling a long distance.

IRIDESCENT (ir-eh-DEH-sent) Having many colors that appear to move and change.

MATE (MAYT) To be a pair for making babies.

REPRODUCE (ree-pruh-DOOS) To have babies.

ROOSTING (ROOST-ing) Going to the place where one rests or sleeps.

URBAN (UR-bun) Having to do with a city.

INDEX

WEB SITES

For Web resources related to the subject of this book,
go to: www.windmillbooks.com/weblinks
and select this book's title.